TAKS Doctor: Strategies for Success (Middle School)

HOLT, RINEHART AND WINSTON

A Harcourt Education Company

Austin • Orlando • Chicago • New York • Toronto • London • San Diego

Photo credit: Cover, Bureau of Economic Geology, The University of Texas at Austin; (bkgd) Texas State Library & Archives Commission

Copyright © by Holt, Rinehart and Winston. All rights reserved. No part of this publication may be reproduced or transmitted in any form or by any means, electronic or mechanical, including photocopy, recording, or any information storage and retrieval system, without permission in writing from the publisher.

Teachers may photocopy complete
pages in sufficient quantities for classroom use only and not for resale.

Printed in the United States of America

ISBN 0-03-067251-1

1 2 3 4 5 6 7 8 9   085   05 04 03 02

Contents

TAKS Doctor: Strategies for Success (Middle School)

I. To The Teacher iv
II. Strategy 1: Critical Reading 1
III. Strategy 2: Answering Multiple-Choice Questions 6
IV. Strategy 3: Memory Devices, Part I 8
V. Strategy 4: Memory Devices, Part II 13
VI. Strategy 5: Visualization 17
VII. Strategy 6: Sequencing 19

To The Teacher

The *TAKS Doctor: Strategies for Success (Middle School)* will give you hands-on strategies that you can use at any time throughout the school year with your students to help them prepare for the Texas Assessment of Knowledge and Skills (TAKS) Grade 8 test. The strategies contained in the *TAKS Doctor: Strategies for Success (Middle School)* utilize content that students are learning in their history courses as well as content that students will be assessed on. The *TAKS Doctor: Strategies for Success (Middle School)* will show you how to implement these strategies in a step-by-step process.

TAKS Doctor: Strategies for Success

Strategy 1: Critical Reading

PURPOSE/RATIONALE

This strategy is designed to help students with the most important skill they need for success on TAKS—critical reading. Students who are critical or analytical readers are more likely to experience success on any assessment.

FOCUS

The teacher may ask students to brainstorm some ways they approach a primary source reading, document, excerpt, or other form of literature when they encounter it. *(Possible answers might be note the title, date, author, and any other information above or below the passage, underline key phrases or words in the passage, underline the main idea, make notes or write questions in the border, etc.)* Tell students that all of these are important, and that more ideas will be added to their thinking with the lesson today.

TEACH

1. Tell students that they will study in Strategy 31 the acronym SOAPS to help them glean information from a reading passage. The strategies they will learn today are similar to SOAPS but may provide more understanding of a difficult reading passage. These strategies are useful as they first approach a reading.

2. Review the following strategies with the class:
   - **Preview**—Previewing allows the students to skim a passage for general understanding before careful reading. As a student quickly skims a text, he or she should quickly note the title, author, date, main idea, and any names mentioned in the reading. The student may ask themselves the 5Ws here—who, what, where, why, when. The purpose is to get an overview of the content.
   - **Contextualize**—Contextualizing allows the student to place the reading in the general time period and locale. After previewing, the student should think back to what he or she knows about history and try to place the reading in the correct historical period and location. Anything the student can remember about that period of time may be helpful in preparing to read critically.
   - **Question**—Questioning before careful reading can help students prepare for deeper understanding. Some questions a student might ask herself or himself about a reading passage are the following:
     - What type of reading is this? (letter, journal, legal document, biography, autobiography, poem, fictional account, etc.)
     - Is the language the sort I would encounter in a modern reading today or is it archaic (old)?
     - What is the general feeling of this passage? (anger, humor, etc.)
     - Is the author a known authority on the subject?

   (If the students cannot answer these questions, it is not a problem as they will get the answers when they carefully read the passage.)

Copyright © by Holt, Rinehart and Winston. All rights reserved.

3. Students are now ready to read the passage with care. This read-through should be done slowly and important points should be underlined or highlighted within the text. Students should underline or box the main idea of the text. Students should reread if the text is very difficult. Finally, students should try to summarize the main points in the reading.

PRACTICE

Students may practice the strategies listed above with the reading on Practice Sheet 1, *The Outbreak of War*, from the **Call to Freedom** booklet of *Readings and Activities*.

CLOSE

Ask students if the strategies used here are similar to the ones they learned in reading classes. *(SQ3R is very close to this approach.)* Explain to students that they will only use these strategies on passages where they need to have an in-depth understanding of what they have read, such as reading passages on the TAKS. Different strategies are used for casual or personal reading.

EXTEND

The teacher may wish to have students practice these strategies several times before they take the Social Studies TAKS. There are many additional readings in the *Readings and Activities* booklet for practice.

Practice Sheet 1

The Outbreak of War

In 1754 George Washington, a lieutenant colonel in the Virginia militia, led 150 soldiers into the Appalachian Mountains to investigate French activity in the region. The passage that follows is from Washington's letter to Robert Dinwiddie, governor of Virginia. The letter describes conflict between the Virginia militia and a group of French soldiers who claimed to be escorting a French ambassador to Williamsburg, the capital of Virginia. As you read the excerpt, consider the conditions under which Washington and his soldiers were fighting.

From our Camp at the Great Meadows [Pa.]
29th of May 1754

Honble [Honorable] Sir . . .

Now Sir, as I have answer'd your Honour's Letter I shall beg leave to acqt [acquaint] you with what has happen'd since I wrote by Mr Gist; I then acquainted [informed] you that I had detach'd [sent] a party of 75 Men to meet with 50 of the French who we had Intelligence [information] were upon their March towards us . . . Abt [About] 9 Oclock the same Night, I receivd an express from the Half King[1] who was incampd with several of His People abt 6 Miles of[f], that he had seen the Tract [tracks] of two French men xing [crossing] the Road and believ'd the whole body were lying not far off . . .—I set out with 40 Men before 10, and was from that time till near Sun rise before we reach'd the Indian's Camp, havg [having] Marched in small path, & heavy Rain, and a Night as Dark as it is possible to conceive—we were frequently tumbling over one another, and often so lost that 15 or 20 Minutes search would not find the path again.

When we came to the Half King I council'd [met] with him, and got his assent to go hand in hand and strike the French; accordingly, himself, Monacatoocha, and a few other Indians set out with us, and when we came to the place where the Tracts were, the Half King sent Two Indians to follow their Tract and discover their lodgment [hiding place] which they did abt half a mile from the Road in a very obscure place surrounded with Rocks. I thereupon in conjunction [agreement] with the Half King and Monacatoocha, formd a disposion [plan] to attack them on all sides, which we accordingly did and after an Engagement of abt 15 Minutes we killd 10, wounded one and took 21 Prisoner's, amongst those that were killd was Monsieur De Jumonville the Commander, Principl Officers taken is Monsieur Druillong and Monsr Laforc, who your Honour has often heard me speak of as a bold Enterprising [ambitious] Man, and a person of gt [great] subtilty [subtlety] and cunning with these are two cadets—These Officers pretend they were coming on an Embassy, but the absurdity of the pretext is too glaring as your Honour will see by the Instructions and summons inclos'd: There Instructions were to reconnoitre [investigate] the Country, Roads, Creeks &ca [etc.] to Potomack; which they were abt to do,

These Enterpriseing Men were purposely choose out [chosen] to get intelligence, which they were to send Back by some brisk dispatches with mention of the Day that they were to serve the Summon's; which could be through no other view[2], than to get sufficient Reinforcements to fall upon us immediately after. This with several other Reasons induc'd [caused] all the Officers to believe firmly that they were sent as spys rather than anything else, and has occasiond my sending them as prisoners, tho they expected (or at least had some faint hope of being continued as ambassadors)....

The Sense of the Half King on this Subject is, that they have bad Hearts, and that this is a mere pretence [falsehood], they never designd [planned] to have come to us but in a hostile manner, and if we were so foolish as to let them go again, he never would assist us in taking another of them....

In this Engagement we had only one Man killd, and two or three wounded, among which was Lieutt [Lieutenant] Waggener slightly—a most miraculous escape, as Our Right Wing was much exposd to their Fire and receivd it all....

Monsiur La-Forc, and Monsieur Druillong beg to be recommend to your Honour's Notice, and I have promis'd they will meet with all the favour that's due to Imprison'd Officers: I have shew'd [shown] all the respect I cou'd to them here, and have given some necessary cloathing by which I have disfurnish'd myself, for having brought no more than two or three Shirts from Wills Ck [Creek] ... I was ill provided to furnish them I am Yr Honour's most Obt Hble Servt [obedient humble servant].

Go: Washington

From *The Papers of George Washington: Colonial Series*, Vol. 1, edited by W. W. Abbot.

PREVIEW THE READING:

What is the title? *The Outbreak of War*

Who is the author? *George Washington*

When was it written? *1754*

Where do the events take place? *Appalachian Mountains in Pennsylvania*

What is the main idea of the reading? *The Virginia militia led by Washington is in conflict with French soldiers.*

CONCEPTUALIZE:

What do I know about what is happening? *This is the era of the French and Indian War in U.S. History. George Washington came into prominence at this time.*

---

[1] American Indian leader

[2] for no other purpose

QUESTION:

What type of reading is this? *A letter*

What type of language is used in the passage? *Old English or archaic*

What is the feeling conveyed by this passage? *Concern*

Is the author a known authority? *Yes*

CAREFUL READING:

Read through the entire article once before highlighting any parts to get the gist of what is said.

Then, as a class, decide what should be highlighted. *(Possible answers include Half King, strike the French, Monsieur De Jumonville, Monsieur Druillong, and Monsr Laforc. These officers pretend they were coming on an Embassy, purposely chosen out to get intelligence, sufficient reinforcements to fall upon us, I have shew'd all the respect I cou'd to them here, etc.)*

What is the main idea? (implied, not directly stated) *Washington and the Virgina militia encountered and fought with hostile French soldiers in the mountains of Pennslyvania.*

Reread if necessary, as this is a difficult document to understand.

Then, have a student summarize in his or her own words what is written here. *(Main idea and supporting details.)*

TAKS Doctor: Strategies for Success

Strategy 2: Answering Multiple-Choice Questions

PURPOSE/RATIONALE

This strategy is designed to make students better test takers. Often students lack skills needed to tackle the multiple-choice item format. With practice, students' confidence should grow and fear of test taking should diminish.

FOCUS

Ask students if they have ever been in such a hurry to do a task that they messed it up and had to start over. (All students will likely nod assent to this question.) Tell them that being in a hurry is the most common error made on multiple-choice questions. Often test takers do not read the question and possible answers several times. Good test takers will tell you that even if they think they know the answer to a question, they will go back and reread the whole item again to be sure they haven't missed something. Today students will work on this skill.

TEACH

1. The teacher may wish to review some general test-taking skills before getting any further into the lesson.
   - Read all parts of a question thoroughly.
   - Apply any knowledge you may have of the time period in question.
   - Use your thinking and reasoning skills.
   - Look for clues, possible answers, or other questions in the question.
   - Come back to difficult questions after answering easier ones first.
   - Usually select the positive rather than the negative response.
   - Search for the broader answer response.
   - If necessary, make educated guesses.

2. The teacher should duplicate the questions from Practice Sheet 1 and give them to students as a quiz. After an appropriate amount of time, the teacher should go over each item with the class and have someone explain what word or words in the stimulus piece, questions, or answer choices helped them the most in selecting the correct answer.

PRACTICE

Teachers may assign any appropriate reading from the *Readings and Activities* booklet for additional practice.

CLOSE

Ask students if they have any other test-taking skills that were not listed above that may help others to do well on multiple-choice tests.

Copyright © by Holt, Rinehart and Winston. All rights reserved.

EXTEND

Teachers should review tests with students throughout the year to continuously keep test-taking skills in mind.

Practice Sheet 1

Massachusetts School Law, 1647

"It being one chief project of the old deluder, Satan, to keep men from the knowledge of the Scriptures, as in former times by keeping them in an unknown tongue, it is therefore ordered that every township in this jurisdiction after the Lord has increased them (in) number to fifty householders, shall then forthwith appoint one within their town to teach all such children as shall resort to him to write and read, whose wages shall be paid either by the parents or masters of such children, or by the inhabitants in general."

_____ **1.** From your knowledge of this period and from the passage above, why was education important in Massachusetts?
  a. to train more men for the ministry
  b. to allow people to read the Bible
  c. to provide an educated workforce
  d. to educate the parents or masters of children

_____ **2.** What was Satan being accused of doing in the following line from the passage? **"as in former times by keeping them in an unknown tongue"**
  a. not allowing the Bible to be translated into English
  b. creating a Bible in his own unknown tongue
  c. deluding people with fake Scriptures
  d. educating men in the wrong tongues

_____ **3.** The above passage was written by and for what group of settlers?
  a. Calvinists
  b. Quakers
  c. Puritans
  d. Huguenots

TAKS Doctor: Strategies for Success

Strategy 3: Memory Devices, Part I

PURPOSE/RATIONALE

This strategy is designed to help students understand how mnemonic—or memory—devices work and to help students analyze primary and secondary sources. These mnemonic devices can be valuable tools for students when they encounter written and visual sources on TAKS. The skills needed to analyze the written and visual pieces that accompany many multiple-choice items will make use of different mnemonic devices.

FOCUS

Ask students if they ever have trouble remembering information. (Most will quickly say "yes.") Ask students if they ever use a mnemonic device (something like a song, rhyme, or acronym) to help them recall information. Have students share some of the mnemonic devices they use with the class.

TEACH

1. Explain to students that mnemonic devices are memory aids that help in recalling important information. Tell students that there are several easy mnemonic devices with which they should be familiar. Some of these are the following:
    - Rhymes
    - Acronyms
    - Visual associations

First, rhymes can help students remember important information. A good example is "In fourteen hundred and ninety-two, Columbus sailed the ocean blue." Some people use rhymes to help them remember the difference between a poisonous coral snake and a harmless king snake—"Red touch yellow, kill a fellow…" or in tightening a bolt or screw—"Righty tighty, lefty loosey." The brain loves rhymes and remembers them when simple facts are long forgotten. This is why advertisers on TV and radio often use this device. It makes it less likely that you will forget their product. Ask students if they can identify the product for "My baloney has a first name, it's O-S-C-A-R"? *(Oscar Meyer)*

Another common mnemonic device is an acronym. Some examples include HOMES for the Great Lakes (Huron, Ontario, Michigan, Erie, Superior) and MY DEAR AUNT SALLY for the order of operations in math (multiply, divide, add, subtract). Using acronyms will be the focus of this strategy lesson.

The last device is a visual association in which mental pictures are used to remember lists or large amounts of information. Students may be interested in knowing that some people have tried to memorize the entire Bible or other long documents using mental pictures. The former Ohio State All-American basketball player and NBA star, Jerry Lucas, astounded his college roommate, John Havlicek, by constantly making As on tests while John struggled. Jerry used mental pictures to remember crucial information. He is known even today as Doctor Memory. Using visual aids is the focus of the Strategy 4 lesson.

Copyright © by Holt, Rinehart and Winston. All rights reserved.

2. Tell students that today they will be learning two acronyms that will help them analyze information on the TAKS test. The acronyms are **SOAPS** for written pieces and **OPTIC** for visual pieces of information. We'll begin with SOAPS.

S	**Subject –**
O	**Occasion –** (or Time)
A	**Audience –**
P	**Purpose –**
S	**Speaker –** (or Author)

Use the SOAPS technique with students on the following primary source that might easily be found on the eighth-grade Social Studies TAKS.

The Emancipation Proclamation
President Abraham Lincoln

"On the first day of January, in the year of our Lord one thousand eight hundred sixty-three, all persons held as slaves within any State, or designated part of a State, the people whereof shall then be in rebellion against the United States, shall be then, thenceforth and forever free; and the Executive Government of the United States, including the military and naval authorities thereof will recognize and maintain the freedom of such persons, and will do no acts to repress such persons, or any of them, in any efforts they may make for their actual freedom."

S	**Subject** –	Freeing the slaves
O	**Occasion** – (or Time)	Civil War Era, 1863
A	**Audience** –	All citizens of the United States and slaves
P	**Purpose** –	To undo the wrong of slavery and to help the Union war effort
S	**Speaker** – (or Author)	President Lincoln

By analyzing a document using **SOAPS**, students will be prepared for any difficult questions that could be asked about it.

The second acronym is **OPTIC**.

O	**Overview** –
P	**Parts** –
T	**Title** –
I	**Interrelationship** –
C	**Conclusion** –

Have students examine the political cartoon shown below of President Jackson depicted as a king, and analyze it using **OPTIC**. The cartoon may also be found on page 391 of *Call to Freedom*. (You can also use this strategy with a different political cartoon or another type of visual.)

O	**Overview –**	President Jackson dressed as royalty.
P	**Parts –**	Jackson is wearing the typical clothing of a king, he is holding a veto sign, he is standing on the Constitution and a U.S. bank document, and there is a throne behind him.
T	**Title –**	King Andrew
I	**Interrelationship –**	Jackson may use the veto to increase his presidential powers; he seems to think the Constitution and Bank are not worth much; and he may think he has the powers of a king rather than a president.
C	**Conclusion –**	President Jackson probably uses his veto powers as well as other powers to go beyond his Constitutional authority.

By thinking through the parts of a visual using **OPTIC,** students deepen their understanding of the item being analyzed.

PRACTICE

Have students try using the SOAPS and OPTIC mnemonic devices as they work through the *TAKS Every Day!* activities.

CLOSE

Have students share with a partner something that has been easy for them to remember because of some mnemonic device (e.g., the black "check sign" for Nike or the slogan "Just Do It"). After a few minutes, ask several students in the class to share their answers with the larger group.

EXTEND

Have students develop their own mnemonic device for the 10 amendments in the Bill of Rights or the 13th, 14th, and 15th Amendments.

TAKS Doctor: Strategies for Success

Strategy 4: Memory Devices, Part II

PURPOSE/RATIONALE
This is another strategy to help students remember crucial information by means of visual mnemonic devices. This is the second part of the lesson on mnemonics.

FOCUS
Remind students that they have already studied some devices to help them remember important information. They used rhymes and songs as well as acronyms to retrieve information from their memories. Now we want to try one more mnemonic device—visual associations—to help students remember historical information. To show students what this device is, ask them to follow your instructions and close their eyes. Then ask them to **not,** repeat, **not** picture a baby elephant in their minds. Wait a few seconds and explain to them they could not help themselves. Everyone in the class, including the teacher, **did** picture a baby elephant in their minds. This is because a great deal of information is stored in picture form in the mind. Students cannot help but see the picture when a word with which they are very familiar is read or spoken. Today we will see if this works for students in retaining information.

TEACH

1. Remind students that mnemonic devices are memory aids that help in recalling important information. Tell students that they will work with one last device today—visual associations.

2. A visual association is a mental picture used to remember lists or large amounts of information. Remind students about Jerry Lucas and his efforts. (This information is available in the first mnemonics lesson.)

3. There are several techniques used to form pictures. One is to identify a place in the classroom where you will always place the first item to remember. Ask students to look to the right front of the classroom. If there is a bulletin board or a chalkboard, that should be Place 1. (They will continue clockwise around the room for additional places.) Then they will want to picture the first item they want to remember. Let's say they need to remember the first five presidents of the U.S. At Place 1, try to find a way to remember George Washington. (Tell students that the brain remembers funny or strange pictures easily so we'll try for that.) Look at the name "Washington" and try to break it down into syllables for pictures. *Washing* is pretty simple if we picture a barefoot old man washing a pair of socks. To add detail to the picture have the man washing the socks use a large, square, ton weight as a washboard. *Ton* is written right along the top of the square weight. Now in your mind's eye you should see the person scrubbing a pair of socks against a ton weight. What is the name you must remember? "Washington." Now, one more detail. We need to remember "George." How about if we have the person washing the socks on the ton weight just ready to fall off into a gorge? The washer is barely hanging on to the ton weight as he washes the socks. Okay, now picture the whole thing in your mind's eye—an old man washing socks against a

ton weight just ready to fall into a gorge. So who are we trying to remember? George Washington. Open your eyes and put that picture from your mind on the place you set up as Place 1. Can you see it right there in your mind?

4. Now try John Adams, the second president. Find Place 2 in the classroom together, and then form a mental picture for John Adams. Picture an outdoor bathroom like people in the country used to use—a *john,* and put a crescent moon on it for detail. Okay, now we want something for "Adams." How about putting 3 Ms down the door with a plus sign. We will *add* Ms on the front of the *john*—John Adams. Okay, now put that image in your mind as you look at Place 2. Try to clearly see it in that spot. (The teacher may wish to draw this on the board if students seem to not know what a john looks like.)

5. Try the third president—Thomas Jefferson. Find Place 3 in the classroom. We need a visual image for "Jefferson." In medieval times, kings were entertained by court **jesters.** Jesters dressed in silly hats and shoes as well as bloomers for pants. Picture one of these silly characters pointing to his son who is about half his size. Can you see the jester's son? Jefferson! Now let's think about "Thomas." Have the jester and his son dance on a drum—a tom-tom. Think of the beat tom-tom-tom-tom in your mind. Now picture this again—the jester dancing on the tom-tom pointing to his son and see if Thomas Jefferson comes to mind. Put him mentally in place 3 in the classroom.

6. Time to review. Look at place 1 and see if you can remember the image for that place. (Most will remember but some will need additional practice to remember the man washing his socks at the gorge.) Next move to Place 2 and ask what mental image they see there. Again remind those who cannot quickly see the john with the *m*'s to add on the door that this is the image for John Adams. Then Place 3 should come back quickly, as we just placed the jester and his son on the tom-tom drums. Tell students that going back and remembering the image is what we call rehearsal for the memory. Most people will need to rehearse the picture several times before it is fully in their minds when they look at the spot in the classroom.

7. Now move to Place 4 and the president—James Madison. "Madison" is fairly easy to remember if you have a man looking angrily down at his son. He is "mad at son" or Madison. Work on "James" now. Have the son hold a length of chain in each hand. "Chains Mad at son" or James Madison. Remember that the more ridiculous the association, the better the brain is at remembering it. Now place it on Place 4 and close your eyes to see the man and his son who is holding a chain in each hand. You can even make up a story about what he was doing with the chains that made his father mad at him if it will help you remember the picture. You could see a bicycle in the background with a missing chain and imagine that the son removed the chain from his bike and then broke it in half. Does that help anyone see the picture more clearly? Stories help many of us with memory.

8. Place 5 in the classroom will have James Monroe. This one will be easier as we'll use *chains* again for "James." This time picture a man rowing a boat on a lake but instead of oars he has stiff chains to row the boat. Can you see man row with chains? "Chains man row" or James Monroe. Again, ask students to go to Place 5 and see the man rowing across the lake.

9. Next, have the students use scratch paper for a quiz. Ask them, place by place, to remember the image and write the name of the president it brings to mind. (Do this slowly so that students have time to conjure up each image.) Did using the places in the room to remember the first five presidents help them? (Have students check each other's answers after a few minutes.)

10. Tell students that they can remember lots of different things using the same places in the room but with different images for different information.

PRACTICE

The teacher may want to assign one of the 13 original colonies to a pair of students to develop an image for practice. If the class has more than 26 students, some colonies will be done by two pairs. (This will take about ten minutes to develop, and then each group will share it's picture with the class (another ten minutes). The teacher may wish to place the images on the places around the room if the founding order of the colonies is part of the lesson.

EXTENSION

The teacher may wish to try one more way to remember a list of events or people that students have to know in some order. Here goes! Many people attach a picture to a number and then put an image on the picture. Let's see how this works.

- one—bun
- two—shoe
- three—tree
- four—door
- five—hive
- six—sticks
- seven—heaven
- eight—crate
- nine—pine
- ten—pen

First, picture what the object attached to the number looks like in your mind's eye. One—bun is a big hamburger bun. Two—shoe is an unusual shoe. It could be a very high-heeled shoe or a Shaquille O'Neal-sized tennis shoe. (Each student should picture these objects the way they want to see them.) Three—tree might be a tree with no leaves or a fluffy billowing tree. Four—door may be a safe's door or any other door the student sees. Five—hive should be a beehive. Six—sticks might be a package of switches or two sticks crossed. Seven—heaven might be billowing clouds in a blue sky. Eight—crate might be a packing box made of wood. Nine—pine should be an evergreen with pine cones on it. Ten—pen might be an animal pen. (The teacher will want to quiz students several times on the images attached to the numbers and explain that students can continue as high as they wish to attach an image to a number, depending on the length of the list to be remembered.) The teacher might then wish to demonstrate her memory for the first ten by asking students to brainstorm a list of 10 grocery items for her to remember. As the students offer an item for number 1, like potatoes, the teacher should mentally put the potatoes on the bun for number 1. The picture should be ridiculous, such as a ten-pound sack with dirty potatoes between a hamburger bun with the top of the bun about to fall off. (Remember that the brain loves novelty and will remember a picture like that very quickly. Animation like the wobbling of the top of the bun only helps the memory come back.) Continue listing items on the board as students suggest them, then mentally put them on the number images. Two might be milk and the teacher could remember the milk spilling out of the shoe as it is being poured into it. Finally, erase the board and try to list all ten items in the order given by students. Don't be afraid—it is easy to remember using mental images.

Next, let one student make up a list of things for a partner to try to remember after the list is taken away. Then, reverse the process so each student gets a chance to practice the technique.

Finally, have students take the images of the presidents from the places in the room and put them on the images attached to numbers. George Washington would be on the hamburger bun, Adams on the tip of the shoe, and so on. (This technique is essentially the same as placing, but it allows for a larger number of things to be remembered.)

TAKS Doctor: Strategies for Success

Strategy 5: Visualization

PURPOSE/RATIONALE

This strategy is designed to help students understand how visualizing specific maps of the U.S. can help them with TAKS. Students who can see general shapes and locations in their minds should be more successful on a variety of questions they could encounter on TAKS.

FOCUS

The teacher may ask students if they could draw a map of the state of Texas from memory. Ask students to do this without looking at a map. Ask them to try to place Dallas, Houston, and El Paso on the map. (The teacher may have students check their renditions of Texas an actual map to see how close they were.) If desired, the teacher may show students how to make a rough map of Texas using their left hands. A student should hold out the left hand with the thumb sticking straight up. The thumb represents the panhandle of Texas. Next, the forefinger of the hand should be pointed outward at a right angle to the thumb with the bottom three fingers bent into the palm of the hand from the knuckles. Ask them if they can see a very rough shape of Texas. Explain that this hand shape doesn't show the southern border of Texas very well, but it does approximate the panhandle, northern, and eastern boundaries.

TEACH

1. The teacher may wish to have students look at the physical map of the U.S. in the textbook on pp. A2 and A3. Explain that the U.S. is shaped roughly like a rectangle with an irregular "V" missing where the Great Lakes are located on the northern border and with land extensions beyond the rectangle in New England, Florida, and Texas. Also, have students notice that the West coastline bulges slightly outward from the rectangle. Then, have them look at the East coastline and notice that it bulges in the middle and has several peninsulas and islands on its northern part. Ask students to trace the boundaries of the U.S. with their fingers as the teacher talks about each area. Have students try to sketch the outline of the U.S. after this discussion with as few "peeks" as possible at the map in the textbook.

2. Then, using the map in the text again, have students look at the location of the Appalachian Mountains (roughly northeast from the state of Georgia to the state of Maine.) Also, have them locate the Rocky Mountains and note that these mountains run from the northern section of New Mexico northwest to the border of the U.S. and Canada. Explain that Canada also has the Rocky Mountains, but we're concerned with only the U.S. for this lesson. Ask them to run their fingers over the locations of both these mountain ranges on the map in the textbook. Then, have students try to draw these mountain ranges into their sketched maps from memory.

3. Next, have students locate the Great Lakes and find the only one completely within the U.S. (The other four lakes serve as borders between Canada and the U.S.) Ask the students to trace the locations of these with their fingers, then try to place the five

lakes on their sketched maps without looking back at the text map.

4. Finally, ask students to find New Orleans on a map of the U.S. (halfway between the peninsulas of Florida and Texas). Explain that this is the mouth of the Mississippi River, the longest river in the U.S. Have students trace with their fingers the Mississippi River from New Orleans northward almost to the border with Canada. Next, have them trace the large rivers that empty into the Mississippi from their sources in the Appalachians (Ohio River) or the Rockies (e.g., Missouri and Arkansas Rivers). This is an excellent time to explain to students that most rivers begin in the mountains or highlands. The specific area is called the "source" of a river. Rivers usually empty into a larger body of water (ocean, sea, another river, lake, etc.), which is called the mouth of the river. Explain that the Rockies are known as the Continental Divide in the U.S. because most rivers run eastward and westward from their sources in these mountains. Now, have students draw the Mississippi River from memory on their maps. (They may also add tributaries if the teacher wishes.)

5. At this point, the teacher may wish to give students a few minutes to correct any major flaws they have on their sketched maps. Ask students to keep these in notebooks or other safe places for use in another lesson.

PRACTICE

After a few days, have students try to draw another map of the U.S. from memory, including mountain ranges and rivers.

CLOSE

Wait a few days and then ask students to close their eyes and see the map of the U.S. in their minds. Can they see the locations of the Great Lakes? Can they see the peninsulas of Florida and Texas? Where are the Appalachian Mountains? Where are the Rockies? Where is New Orleans and the mouth of the Mississippi River? What does the West Coast of the U.S. look like? *(slightly bulging)* What does the East Coast look like? *(bulges in the middle with a few small peninsulas and islands in the north)*

EXTEND

The teacher may want to continue doing mapping from memory as with the major physical features of the U.S. The next exercise may have students use their first map to identify the 13 colonies (New England, Middle, and Southern), the areas added to the U.S. through Manifest Destiny, important locations in the west like Salt Lake City and Sutter's Mill, the Mason-Dixon Line for the Civil War division, or any other mapping that the teacher deems important.

Hint: Always have the students trace the areas that need to be remembered with their fingers on the textbook map before they attempt to place them on a map using only what they remember.

TAKS Doctor: Strategies for Success

Strategy 6: Sequencing

PURPOSE/RATIONALE

This strategy is designed to help students understand how sequencing events and understanding chronology can help them with TAKS. Students with a sense of when events in U.S. history occurred should be more successful on a variety of questions they could encounter on TAKS.

FOCUS

The teacher may ask students to think back to Texas history and put these events in the order in which they occurred.

Texas statehood

Austin's colonization of Texas

Texas independence

Mexican control of Texas

Discovery of oil in Texas

(This should only take a few minutes and can be done as a pair-share activity.) The teacher may ask one group to share to see if the class agrees or disagrees with the placement.

TEACH

1. The teacher may wish to refresh students' minds on the term *chronology*—the arrangement of events in time order. Explain that most history books are organized in chronological order, the order in which the events actually occurred. This organization helps students to understand cause and effect and other relationships of events.

2. Then, have students turn to the time line on pp. 118–119 of their textbook. Explain that time lines are useful for many reasons. They provide a visual organizer for chronology, they can show order of events, they can show multiple events occurring at the same time, and they can help students understand relationships among events. Students may need to be reminded that the time sequences on a time line have to follow a pattern. Time lines may show short periods of time or long periods of time, but each segment of a time line must be equal to every other segment. For example, a time line of the entire history of the U.S. may be divided into 20 year segments, e.g., 1600–1620, 1620–1640, and so on. Each segment **must** be 20 years. (Students often make the mistake of dividing time lines into different segments of time, such as one segment at 10 years and another at 20, etc.) A major event of short duration, such as the Civil War, may be shown on a time line divided into single year segments to allow space for many events in each segment.

3. Using dates and time lines are techniques to help the student sequence events. Students need to have a time line in their minds when they approach TAKS. It may be helpful if the teacher puts the following time line on the board or in the fronts of

Copyright © by Holt, Rinehart and Winston. All rights reserved.

student notebooks and continuously ties events into the time line. Before TAKS is given, have students reproduce the time line from memory along with any major events that the teacher wishes to include.

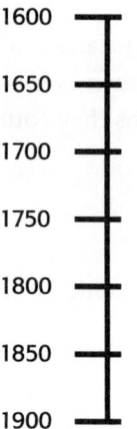

4. Tell students that they will be sorting information from cards into chronological order for their lesson today.

PRACTICE

The teacher will need to make several copies of the events on Practice Sheet 1. Next, cut the sheet into squares and shuffle them before giving students the cards to put in order. (Laminate if desired.) Then, have students in pairs sort the attached cards into chronological order. They may use the text to get dates to help them if necessary.

CLOSE

Have students design a set of cards for different events for other classmates to put into order or to place on time lines. They may make cards for the 13 colonies, territorial additions to the U.S. after 1800, wars, individuals from various periods of time, and so on.

EXTEND

If Tom Snyder software is available, the students may practice putting a series of events on a time line, or the teacher may wish to have students create time lines for whatever is being studied in the class. (Multiple practices will be needed for students to develop a sense of time as this is difficult for children in this age group.)

Copyright © by Holt, Rinehart and Winston. All rights reserved.

Practice Sheet 1

Jamestown is founded.

Mayflower Compact is agreed upon by Pilgrims.

Puritans settle in Massachusetts.

Maryland is founded as a haven for Catholics.

Oglethorpe founds Georgia.

English take over Dutch Colonies.

Slavery begins in the Southern colonies.

Plymouth is settled.

Dutch settle in New Amsterdam.

The Carolinas are chartered.

Penn settles in Pennsylvania.

Triangular trade routes are established.

Practice Sheet 2

TIME LINE FOR STUDENTS

Time Segments

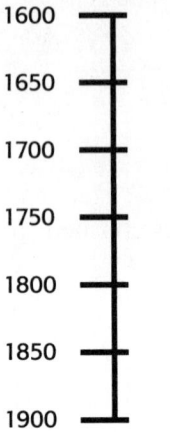

Eras

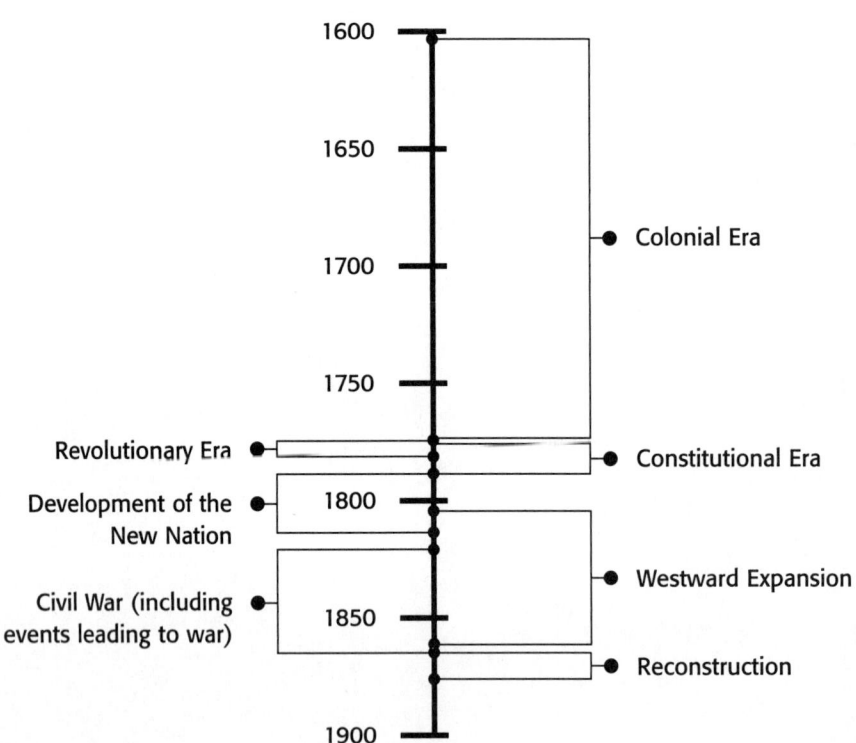